Seeking
Effective Sch
for Africa
Ch

Strategies for Teachers
and School Managers

By Bunyan Bryant
and
Alan H. Jones

Seeking Effective Schools
for African American Children:
Strategies for Teachers
and School Managers

By Bunyan Bryant and Alan H. Jones

Copyright 1993 by Caddo Gap Press

Published by **Caddo Gap Press**
    3145 Geary Boulevard, Suite 275
    San Francisco, California 94118
    (415) 750-9978

Price - $11.95

ISBN 1-880192-01-2
Library of Congress Catalog Card Number 92-73154

Publisher's Cataloging in Publication
(Prepared by Quality Books Inc.)

Bryant, Bunyan I.
    Seeking effective schools for African American children :
strategies for teachers and school managers / Bunyan Duncan and
Alan H. Jones.
    p. cm.
    Includes bibliographical references.
    Preassigned LCCN: 92-73154.
    ISBN 1-1880192-01-2

    1. Afro-American students--United States. 2. Academic
achievement--United States. 3. Teaching.   I. Jones, Alan H. II.
Title.

LC2771.B79 1993   371'.0089960'73
                                          QBI93-714

Contents

Introduction

The term "effective schools" has become the rallying cry of American education in the last two decades of the Twentieth Century, symbolizing a presumed desire to fulfill the traditional promise that American public schooling will serve as the pathway to success for all of the nation's children. Yet, as ongoing evaluations of American educational institutions and comparisons with those of other modern nations contiue to show, the actual "effectiveness" of our schools as measured by the achievements of many of our students does not fulfill this promise. A regular feature of such periodic reports has been the clear documentation that American public schools almost without exception fail at all levels to meet the needs of African American students..

The purpose of this volume is to explore such phenomena, to discuss the realities of contemporary education for African American students in our schools, and to offer a series of suggestions to teachers and school managers for bringing about that desired "effectiveness" for this particular segment of our schools' broad and diverse population.

The Social and Economic Context

Modern American schools operate in a social, political, and economic context of considerable uncertainty. Rapidly changing international political realities, the continuing explosion of development and use of technology in all aspects of modern life, and rhetoric about the importance of education far stronger than the fiscal priorities actually given to American schools serve to create conditions in which it is increasingly difficult to bring about the promised "effectiveness" for any group of students.

Internationally, ending the Cold War has helped facilitate major political and economic disruptions and change in Eastern Europe and the former Soviet Union, with repercussions in many other parts of the world. American military spending, a significant factor in our nation's fiscal priorities since World War II, continued to increase during the Reagan and Bush Administrations despite the cooling of international tensions, resulting in near bankruptcy of the economies on both sides of the former Iron Curtain. In today's downward economy, marked by bank failures, widespread industrial layoffs, near double-digit unemployment, greater need but less funds for welfare, spiriling medical costs and inadequate health insurance, and the departure of businesses and jobs from our shores to other nations where costs (i.e., wages) are less, the ultimate priority for effective education of all children remains highly questionable.

The ever-expanding economic pie that was part of the evolution of American society through the 1960s no longer exists. Today's reality is instead a pervasive competitiveness for decent employment and an acceptable standard of living. A belief in supply-side economics has led our government in the face of these challenges to cut taxes, seeking to provide corporations and wealthier citizens with the funds to make additional investments that are expected to stabilize the economy, seeking to increase both employment and profits; but the net effect has apparently been the opposite. Money saved from corporate taxes is used instead to buy or merge with already existing corporations, not to stimulate new growth and economic development. The result has been a decrease, not an increase, in jobs.

This pattern must also be considered in the context of two other factors: as automation increases, so too does the loss of employment opportunities; and under the Reagan and Bush Administrations a breaking and dismantling of labor unions was fostered and encouraged, forcing workers in many areas to accept wage concessions. The overall impact of these forces on the poorer segments of American society has been catastrophic—wages are lower in terms of real purchasing power, unemployment is up, and millions of families are welfare-dependent. This entire under-society within America has been relegated to a situation that can only be marked by anger, despair, and uncertainty.

It is ironic that the United States found the money and political will to fight a war in the Persian Gulf, but cannot muster similar money or political will to fight a war on poverty and injustice here at home. In the name of national security and as a so-called defender of democracy, our nation spent billions of dollars to defend Kuwait, a country that never had a true democracy and one that has been cited for numerous human rights violations, particularly during the post-war era of the Persian Gulf.

The threat to national security is not from without; rather it is from within, as the poor and minorities cry out in their pain for social and economic justice. The deepening gap between the "haves" and the "have nots" threatens our national equilibrium and the tranquility of the state.

National security would better be viewed as equal access to education, employment, health care, and a decent place to live.

Implications for Education

What does all of this mean for education? A primary consideration is that the supply-side economic policies of the nation are rapidly creating a two-tier society. Much has been written over the past several decades about the educational problems of economically disadvantaged students, and particularly those who are racial or ethnic minorities. But if we think that the educational crisis of the African American child is serious now, it is nothing compared to what the future will unveil if our national economic trends continue.

If the United States continues its present social and economic patterns through the year 2000, without improvements in our educational system to address the needs of economically disadvantaged children, we will surely be facing a disabling societal crisis. The percentage of school children coming from poor and minority backgrounds will soon be approaching half of our student population, while adequately-paying employment will be less and less available to those who complete their education, and the numbers of students—African American and white, as well as others—who fail to achieve even minimal literacy will serve only to expand the under class. That such conditions will further exacerbate conflicts between the races, as well as between economic classes, seems almost certain.

As the various minority populations in America continue to grow, the United States will undoubtedly become a nation featuring the most diverse society on the face of the earth. With such diversity, there will have to be increased understandings and a more open and just society if we are to remain socially viable. Facing the challenge of diversity can strengthen rather than weaken our country; facing diversity has the power to release more creative potential than has previously been available in any society.

Becoming Proactive

Given this analysis, it would appear incumbent upon educators who work in schools with significant proportions of economically-disadvantaged students, and particularly African American students, to work far more effectively at assisting those "at risk" students to become genuinely competitive educationally, and thus economically. As the foreign markets have become more competitive, many American corporations have sought to meet this challenge through new management and training techniques.

It is time for American schools to do the same—to become more proactive and assertive in efforts to meet the needs of poor and minority students.

It is long past time for our schools to mount an educational effort that will make African American students competitive with their white counterparts. It is not simply an issue of race, or a problem that resides in the African American community alone. Indeed, the United States would dramatically increase its ability to function both commercially and diplomatically throughout the world if it would educate its African American youngsters to effectively assume roles in corporate and governmental leadership.

The majority of the world population is that of people of color. The appearance of African Americans in significant commercial and diplomatic positions within the United States, in at least a fair proportion to the number of African Americans within the population of our nation, would constitute a statement about equity and fairness that could only enhance our standing in the international community.

Even more important, perhaps, is the future impact on our domestic economy. Labor trends indicate that by the year 2000, one out of every three working people in American will be of African American descent—if, indeed, we are able to control unemployment and successfully prepare all members of our society for gainful jobs. There are two messages here: first, if a significant portion of jobs in our economy is to be held by minorities, then it behooves us to provide the best education possible so that such employees can obtain and function effectively in such positions; and, second, if we fail to accomplish such ends, the economic drain of our unemployment costs and social security, a system already on the verge of bankruptcy, will destroy our society from within.

The Political Will to Help All Achieve

Accepting the fact that many African American youngsters, along with even more white children, face debilitating environmental conditions caused by homes and neighborhoods marked by poverty, it is more than ever incumbent upon our schools to create settings in which all children can learn. While it is also true that differences in the financial viability of neighborhoods, cities, and even regions of the nation are reflected in the funding available to operate local schools, we must not let the notion that money is the only key to effective schooling prevent us from taking bold educational steps. Despite discrepancies in financial allocations among our nation's schools, and despite the fact that large proportions of students in many buildings come from poor and minority backgrounds, there are many schools in which the students, teachers, and managers have come together to foster and build a learning environment where students have achieved regardless of economic or racial background.

The bottom line is that all students can and will achieve, if educators have the political will to assist those students. African American students can and will achieve and compete equally with their white counterparts, if the teachers and managers of schools with significant African American enrollments have the political will to make that happen. It is political will, not new technology or new scientific breakthroughs or vast increases in school funding, that is most important—although increases in funding are certainly needed as well.

This political will must take the form of new directions and new leadership among teachers and school managers who work with African American students. Although American educators have had the knowledge—the data about what makes effective schools—at hand for more than a decade now, in very few schools has the time been set aside for teachers to engage themselves and each other in strategic educational planning. School staffs seldom make an effort to put into practice what has been gleaned from research about those schools where African American children have succeeded.

Instead, too often, teachers are strangers to one another within their own building. They seldom take the time or have the desire to work together cooperatively in solving critical social and academic problems. They seldom have the opportunity to share the pain of working with students who are failing both academically and socially, or to exchange the success stories that they do have. They garner neither emotional support or professional growth from one another.

Ultimately, it is a question of leadership, of political will. School principals and managers, working with teachers, must break through these traditional patterns of isolation and neglect. The time must be found and made available for teachers to engage one another, to exchange ideas and strategies, and to participate in genuine educational planning and problem-solving. Shared leadership between school managers and teachers is critical to both their own professional growth and the ultimate educational environment offered students.

Looking at Strategies

What is being encouraged here is not so much a new educational breakthrough, or the development of something never before done in any school, but rather a careful, thoughtful, strategic review of what we already know about effective education, and the application of that knowledge to those schools where the task at hand is to effectively educate African American students. The strategies in question have evolved from educational efforts in American schools over several generations, and have been polished by recent research in what has come to be called the "effective schools movement."

Relevant information is presented here around five major criteria that the late Ronald Edmonds, a prominent African American leader of the effective schools movement and a principal spokesperson for the application of such knowledge to the education of African American children, set forth in his writings now more than a decade ago (Edmonds, 1979). He suggested that in order for schools to achieve, they must possess at minimum the following criteria: (1) Strong administrative leadership; (2) A climate of expectation, in which no children are allowed to fall below minimum but efficacious levels of achievement; (3) An atmosphere which is orderly without being rigid; (4) Pupil acquisition of basic skills takes precedence over all other activities, with energy and resources diverted from other areas to this key purpose; and (5) Pupil progress is continually monitored, so that everyone involved can remain constantly aware of such progress in relation to instructional objectives.

In this volume, around each of Edmonds' five criteria, we have grouped some key problems, major questions, and an overview of information currently available about effective schools. While it has not been possible to go into great detail in this text, it is hoped that the information provided will serve as a stimulus for substantive discussion about how teachers and school managers can make their schools effective for all children, with particular attention to African American students. It should be remembered that there are no right or wrong answers to many of the questions and issues raised. Rather, there is a wide variety of information, instructional strategies, and educational experience that should be considered as prospective means for teachers and principals in each school to create a plan and a program that will foster success for all children.

The thrust of this volume is aimed at schools with significant enrollments of African American students—schools that in all likelihood must struggle against issues of race as well as the impact of poverty. At the same time, educational issues, problems, and strategies are similar for all schools, since the process of seeking school effectiveness is simply a matter of degree, depending upon social, economic, and political conditions in each school community that either foster or work against such effectiveness.

Whatever the school, whatever the community, it is imperative that teachers and school managers break away from traditional patterns of isolation, and join together in meeting the educational needs of their students. Presented here are a wide range of topics and challenges that must be dealt with by teachers and principals in regular, face-to-face meetings. These are posed here primarily in the context of schools working with significant enrollments of African American students, since current social trends in America suggest that this may be the most critical and challenging segment of our educational community for implementation of the principles of the effective schools literature.

Notes

Notes

Criteria I:
Strong Administrative Leadership

The first of Edmonds' five criteria for effective schools is strong administrative leadership. Schools which possess such strong leadership will, by example, tend to have students who will succeed, regardless of race or social class backgrounds. Studies of instructionally effective inner-city schools, based upon national norms, have demonstrated that strong principals are important in setting the tone of the school, in deciding on educational strategies, and in allocating the resources to get the job done.

The problem of educating students belongs essentially to the school, not to society at large, although it is important that society support the educational mission of the school. Within that school, if students are not achieving, the problem more often than not is inadequate leadership.

The concept of cultural deprivation, a set of theories suggesting that African American inner-city youngsters could not succeed in school, has served as an excuse for the failures of teachers and school leaders for several decades now. More recent research, however, has revealed the falseness of such theories.

It is not that the cultural circumstances of students are irrelevant, but simply that effective school leadership can provide the atmosphere, the motivation, and the models by which all children can achieve and succeed in school.

Administrators as Change Agents

The model under which most school administrators have been trained, and have served throughout their careers, involves a person in a position of authority who gives directions to teachers and students in accordance with preconceived educational goals. It is their role to give directions which will lead to order out of the daily chaos and turmoil of the school.

Given the multitude of societal problems that now impinge on our children, and likely on future generations if prevailing patterns are not reversed, it appears that this traditional notion of a principal or school leader who simply gives directions is obsolete. It is idealistic to think that contemporary school administrators can set things straight simply by directing teachers and students in a manner that may have worked a few decades ago.

Instead, the effective school administrator—now and in the future—must have direct impact upon the teaching and educational achievements of students in that school. Rather than standing alone or above it all, as school principals have traditionally done, the modern school leader must get involved with the teachers and students, with the community, and with all of the potential resources and services available. The principal must mobilize all of these parties, and focus resources in ways that actually improve the quality of education.

Such administrators break the shackles of the past, moving away from the confines of political conformity. They are visionary and future-oriented. They not only possess images of the high potential to be reached by teachers and students in their school, but they operate in ways that assure the constant feedback that both motivates and measures organizational change and educational renewal. As effective administrators examine the trends of the past and the present, they use such information to create images of educational futures in their schools and districts. As leaders they are not tied down either by tradition or the realities of the present. The effective school administrator for today and tomorrow is a change agent.

Definition of an Effective Administrator

A more specific definition of this effective administrator follows:
     (1) Has organizational goals clearly and precisely defined;
     (2) Accomplishes what one sets out to do;
     (3) Seldom expresses negative feelings or generates negative feelings on the part of others;

(4) Is rational in all proceedings; and

(5) Exposes images of the future. (Erlandson, 1976)

Action Questions

Current and prospective school administrators are encouraged to use this definition as a tool to measure that with which you are familiar. How do you stack up against those five criteria? Have you yourself been able to operate in these ways as an administrator, or have you seen others who have done so successfully? What are your strengths and weaknesses when compared to this definition?

You should also think about this definition in a broader sense. What are the resources in your school district which could be used to realize the criteria and characteristics listed? What could be done to enhance quality education? And what are the areas of resistance or constraint in your district and your school which keep you or other administrators from becoming this sort of change agent?

In the final analysis, the key questions are: How can school administrators become futurists? How can they facilitate school change? How can they assure that teachers and the school programs are as effective as possible, and that student achievement is maximized for all? And what other questions should be asked? As you think about such possibilities, yet other challenges will arise that you will need to tackle as well.

The Politics of Evaluation

The operation of effective schools requires some form of evaluation, since without evaluation it will not be possible to know just how effective the educational program is and how much the students are achieving, either individually or as a group. Thus, some form of planned evaluation must be built into the educational program of an effective school.

At the same time, it must be realized that evaluation is a political thing: it is political from the point of view of the teacher, since evaluation of the program and the students is in reality an evaluation of the effectiveness of the teacher; it is political from the point of view of the students, since evaluation involves some judgment about how well they are doing; it is political from the point of view of the administrator, since the data are being collected as a means of justifying the current program or to develop information to propose some change; and it is political in the eyes of the community, since it provides information by which to judge the operation of the schools.

Thus, when school people speak of evaluations, consultants, special committees, task forces, research projects, and the like, such things always have a political flavor. There is always the potential for change, and for disagreement about directions. Evaluation and change, of course, are not evil in and of themselves; the question is, whose interests will be served? Or whose will be served the most?

Given such political realities, school evaluation must be balanced and, while important, must not be overemphasized. Both positive and negative evaluations should be expected and encouraged, and the results should be juxtaposed to gain a balanced picture. Where possible, the messages from negative evaluations should be addressed and resolved, but not in ways that overshadow or ignore the positive evaluative messages received.

To avoid the potential pitfalls of such questions about evaluation, it is important that the school administrator, as well as interested teachers and other parties in the school, help shape the evaluation and research instruments to be used. Questions should be viewed as statements which condition the subject's response in a certain manner or direction. While one goal of evaluation is to gather relevant and accurate data about the achievements of the school program, it is also important to seek positive feedback.

The outcomes of evaluation will often make the difference between a positive or a negative image of a school or a program. It is therefore important that administrators help determine such outcomes by participating in the development of the research instruments, by contributing questions that will be answered in ways that will ensure fairness and enhance a positive school image. Effective schools thrive off positive images, not negative ones. Teachers, students, support staff, and the community will all lend greater emotional support to a school with a positive image. Evaluation developed at the local level should seek to obtain feedback about any and all positive aspects of each school and program.

In circumstances where national or state level standardized tests are utilized, the political context may be even more complicated. Many such instruments have built-in cultural biases which will provide less than positive results in schools with significant numbers of disadvantaged or minority students. The administrator, however, can often find ways to disaggregate this data to reveal some local success stories, as well as to explain the bias that may be involved in the examination. Once again, the goal is to find and stress the positive feedback that comes from the evaluation, whatever form it may take.

Exercise

For example, in statewide testing, you may find that in your school African American children as a whole have not scored above the average with respect to mathematics or reading at the grade levels tested. On the other hand, you may be able to identify some particular groupings of students, perhaps African American students in a given grade or from a specific church in the community, who scored above the national averages.

This kind of data can then be used to publicize those specific success stories, and to build a more successful image that can be used to motivate all teachers and students towards the testing program next year. Of course, one must never settle for these more limited success stories—the overall goal always is to bring the performance of all students up to acceptable and effective levels.

Some Sample Information

Consider the following information:

Data Set:
An Elementary School Pattern Focusing
on Student Achievement Over Time

School	Reading Percentile		Math Percentile	
	Fall	Spring	Fall	Spring
A	14	16	17	13
B	20	27	27	37
C	51	58	39	41
D	23	70	30	58
E	15	25	17	28

Action Questions

Let's raise some questions about this data. If you were the principal of school A, and the district superintendent of schools asked to speak with you about the reading and mathematics scores for your building, how would you explain the situation? What factors would you need to know? What if you were the principal of school D? How have such significant improvements occurred in your students?

In your experience, how have the politics of testing and evaluation been manifested in your school, your district, and your state? How can such results be used not only to give you some data on achievement, but also to develop a constructive and positive image of your school, your teachers, and your students? Is it dishonest to engage in some analysis and disaggregation of the data in order to look for and publicize the brightest spots?

Seeking Fiscal Equity

The system by which public schools are funded in the United States is replete with inequities. Historically, American schools have been supported primarily by local property taxes, that obviously reflect the wealth, ability, and desire of various local areas to support their schools. Through a pattern of legal challenges of such inherent inequity, and a recognition of the inability of the property tax to adequately fund schools, state governments across the nation have gradually moved to assume some portion of the fiscal responsibility for public schools; currently, on the average, state governments provides about half the funding for schools nationally. However, there are also significant inequities between states in their ability, as well as their political will, to fund education.

Thus, federal support for education has generally been aimed at seeking some equalization among states and localities, with funds made available based primarily upon demonstrated need; but since the federal government appropriates less than 10 percent of all funds spent on education, federal programs have failed to achieve any real equity among local schools.

Many educational observers have documented the significant differences in educational spending between urban, suburban, and rural school districts; typically, it is the urban and rural schools that operate with far less money to spend per student, while suburban schools are far more able to serve their constituency adequately. If funding is not really important in delivering educational effectiveness, as some conservative observers argue, then why does there continue to be such political resistence to reforms that would fully equalize per-pupil spending across schools and districts? Why is there resistance to reducing funding in the suburbs in order to increase it in the more needy urban and rural areas?

Action Questions

Consider the realities of educational funding in the United States. What can you, as a teacher or administrator in a local school system, do about this situation? Should you attempt to get your professional association or some other interested parties to mount a political or legal challenge against such inequities? How would you go about such an effort?

Or should you concentrate your energies on making the best possible use of the funds available to your school? What are some of the strategies you might exercise in this direction? Are there ways to raise additional monies for educational programs in your community?

Living Conditions

In recent years, there has been considerable concern expressed by people of color regarding the frequent use of their communities as waste repositories. Already overburdened by deplorable living conditions, the siting of commercial hazardous waste facilities in communities of color only adds to the mounting social, economic, and political deprivation—now by adding genuinely life-threatening environmental circumstances.

A research report issued by the United Church of Christ Commission for Racial Justice clearly indicates that race is the single most accurate variable identified in association with the location of commercial hazardous waste facilities. In addition, minority and low income communities are often vulnerable to polluting industries, federal Superfund sites, illegal dumping, incinerators, and leaky underground gasoline storage tanks. Those who are the most vulnerable to the siting of such facilities are, typically, those who are least protected by health insurance; they are part of the 37 million people in this country who go unprotected daily. They are the ones who fall to the bottom of any statistical chart of health or other characteristics of social or economic viability.

A Scenario

You are the principal of a school that has been built next to an open area that used to be a landfill. The school's playground is now precisely where the landfill used to be. In addition, there are three chemical plants and two incinerators, one of which is owned by the school district, as well as a sewage treatment plant, all within one-half mile of the school. You have noticed over the years that there has been an increase in student absenteeism due to a variety of illnesses. Some are suffering from respiratory problems, dizziness, and chronically upset stomachs; these become more and more common complaints. You have also observed that the number of students requiring remedial help in academic areas has grown.

In addition, you have just learned that lead poisoning is one of the major environmental health problems in the United States. It is an irreversible condition, attacking the central nervous system, causing impaired thinking, lack of coordination, and other developmental problems. Urban environments in particular are subject to lead from water, lead-based paints, incineration, and concentrated automobile emissions. Even though lead was significantly reduced in gasoline in the 1980s, the emissions of lead from gasoline over the past 50 years have accumulated in the soil, particularly along major transportation corridors. Thus, eight million inner-city children are daily exposed to the dangers of lead poisoning. Indeed, what has been diagnosed in many instances as classic mental retardation is the result of lead poisoning.

Staff from the local ecology center have been trying to get you, as a local school principal, to cut the volume of the school's waste stream by instituting a recycling program. This would reduce the need for incineration. They have also been trying to get you to incorporate an environmental education program into your school's curriculum. While you have been generally receptive to such ideas, you have not given them high priority. On one occasion, however, the ecology center staff gave you one of their reports based on data compiled from the 1992 Environmental Protection

Agency's Toxic Release Inventory. This report shows that the chemical industries and incinerators nationally spew out thousands of tons of arsenic, cadmium, lead, PCBs, mercury, chronium, copper, manganese, dioxins, and other dangerous or potentially dangerous chemicals. Based on this report, you become interested not only in instituting recycling and environmental education, but also in investigating more carefully the immediate environmental safety of your school site in order to ameliorate any unsafe conditions for your students and teachers. The more you study the situation, the more you come to expect that everyone in your school is paying a high price by living and working in this immediate area.

The population of your school is 90 percent African American, and it is located in the poorest neighborhood in the city. Crime and unemployment are high in this area. There are constant problems with discipline, with a lack of student achievement, and with health care in general. Many of the students fail to get adequate dental and medical attention on a regular basis.

All of this is compounded by the fact that you do not have adequate text books or science equipment to implement the school district curriculum. You suspect that the surrounding industries and hazardous waste facilities are the cause of many of the physical problems being experienced by your students. You also know that about 50 percent of the tax support for the local schools comes from the chemical plants, the incinerator, and other privately owned facilities that pollute the area. These industries not only contribute to the tax base, but also to charitable activities such as churches, the United Fund, boy and girl scout troops, the junior football league, etc.; they are obviously concerned about their public image.

Action Questions

As the school principal, how do you respond to this situation? How do you go about getting information that may show that pollutants from these private industrial facilities are having a detrimental impact on students in your school, both physically and academically? How do you organize to get help? Specifically, what do you want the local industries to do? What assistance do you seek? What would be your priorities? Who are the key individuals and agencies you should contact? How can they help with this set of problems?

How can you raise these issues in such a way that your teachers will not simply use the impact of hazardous waste on student achievement as an excuse for lowering their expectations for their students? How do you give teachers, students, and parents hope in the face of such conditions?

How would you go about establishing an environmental education program in this school? How many courses should be involved in such a program? More specifically, how could you institute a water monitoring class to test for chemicals, heavy metals, and fecal coliform bacteria? How could this course use civics, economics, and politics to understand the local conditions? How could computer conferencing involving your students and experts in public health and natural resources contribute to your curriculum? How would you build an effective recycling program? What are some of the other questions to be raised and activities to be undertaken in this situation?

The Administrator as a Focus

These are only a few examples of the many issues and problems that face schools today, and with which the local building administrator must grapple. The point of such examples is to stress the role and value of imaginative, visionary leadership in each school. The administrator does not act alone in this or any other matter; rather, the effective school principal works with the teachers, students, and the community to create and maintain a highly positive image of the school, and works with those same parties to use that image as a motivational force in seeking the highest possible achievement on the part of all students.

Notes

Criteria II:
A Climate of Expectation

> *Edmonds' second criteria for effective schooling involves the creation of a climate of expectation, in which no children are allowed to fall below a minimum yet efficacious level of achievement. An atmosphere which fosters and encourages success and which stresses the self-worth of all students must be generated.*

For schools which serve a significant number of African American students, special steps must often be taken to create and sustain an educational climate that communicates to students an expectation of success. Many strategies are possible; a combination of instruction in African American history and opportunities for students to utilize their talents have often successfully served this self-affirming purpose.

The goal is to provide continuous feedback to students of their self-worth, and to demonstrate that individual self-worth is an outgrowth of a proud social history. Once students respect themselves and their social heritage, it is natural for them to enjoy an improved self-concept, which in turn is a predisposition for stronger and more acceptable levels of academic achievement.

Such support for children's self-growth and social respect must be accompanied in the school by understanding and support on the part of teachers. Ongoing professional development programs for teachers and administrators, coupled with community involvement in support of such educational programs, will foster the necessary climate of expectation in which all children can achieve acceptable levels of academic performance, both according to national norms and in preparation for productive adult lives.

African American History as a Political Statement

Western society as depicted in most textbooks and most school class-rooms is a predominately white story. While this may be true in terms of overall proportions and numbers, the problem with the story as it is too often told is that non-western cultures and non-white peoples who have played a part in western history are depicted, if at all, as less than adequate, as deficient rather than just different. Instead of describing the contributions that other cultures and peoples have made to western civilization, and to the United States in particular, the dominant culture has displayed a white cultural arrogance that systematically portrays African Americans and other people of color as inferior, regularly relegating them to lesser roles.

Discussion of social history in schools, in literature, in the media, and in conversation at all levels of society is a significant part of the culture and heritage of our nation. It impacts all children during their formative years, and assists them in making statements about who they are, and how they feel about themselves. If the goal of our schools and our society is to foster genuine social equality, and to assure achievement and success for all, then we must increase the presentation and appreciation of African American history as a means of improving the self-concept and the academic perfor-mance of African American students.

African American history is not anti-western or anti-white. Rather, it is pro-African American, in that it emphasizes the positive roles and contribu-tions of African Americans and of the overall African American experience. It is simply a matter of balancing the historical record, of demonstrating that not all of the major contributors to our heritage have been white. African American history should be viewed and taught from the political orienta-tion of empowerment; just as our more traditional approach to history has strengthened the self-concept of white children, so will African American history provide such pride for African American students.

In order for African American youngsters to survive and prosper in social environments that are not always friendly, it is important that they be grounded in an historical context that stresses who they are and where they have come from, that they be familiar with a social history that indicates that African Americans have made significant contributions to the larger Ameri-can culture and that African Americans do indeed belong to and belong within this nation. It is, of course, a history that includes severe oppression, of an institutionalized nature, followed by resistance, strife, and gradual change in the social institutions leading to liberation. The ultimate story is one of liberation, and it is that story which must be told effectively in order for African American students to understand their history and find the support and encouragement that will motivate them educationally.

Scenario

As an example of the potential and vital role of African American history, consider for the moment that you are a teacher of African American history in an integrated high school. Most of the students in your class are low-achieving African Americans, with a sprinkling of whites. It is not that the African American students cannot achieve, but they choose not to. They are loud, boisterous, and often intimidating to the white students.

They are taking your course because, as one African American student indicates, "It's a good rap." Students fail to hand in assignments, and they frequently argue among themselves about issues that have little or nothing to do with the subject matter at hand. On any given day, a few of the students will fall asleep in the class. Most of the high-achieving African American students in the school shy away from this course.

Action Questions

What can be done to correct this situation? How can this course be made more interesting for the African American students who now pay it little heed? What can be done to get the students currently in the course to take interest and achieve? What can be done to attract the already high-achieving African American students in the school to take this course?

How can the African American history program be improved and expanded? Are there local resources that can be incorporated into the course? What about getting students to interview their parents, grandparents, or even in some cases their great-grandparents or other relatives? What about finding an historical site to be researched— i.e., is there a building in your city that was used as part of the "Underground Railway"?

How can study skills, reading, writing, and other basics be integrated into the course? If African American history is to be genuinely liberating, what do you need to do to make this goal effective? What kinds of support and assistance do you need from other teachers and from the school administration?

The African American Co-Story

While the emphasis must be on African American history in general, it is important to realize that it is a story of both men and women. Perhaps it should be the African American co-story, rather than either his story or her story, because African American women have played an integral part in the history-making of African Americans in America, as well as throughout the world.

At the same time, a wide variety of observations and reports suggest that both the African American male and female are in a particular state of crisis in America today, a state that may be unparalleled in history. While visible forms of physical oppression may not be evident, the African American male and female suffer from a variety of societal forces often beyond their control. Underemployment, unemployment, drug dependency, homicides, imprisonment, teen pregnancies, low self-esteem, school dropouts, illiteracy, and the lack of other basic skills are all conditions that are becoming the rule rather than the exception for the African American male and female in the United States.

To reverse this perilous trend is at least in large part a role that must be played by our schools. It will take considerable political will on the part of teachers and administrators, and particularly African American educators who can serve as effective role models. While those of us in the field of education are not the cause of this tragic condition, we must take responsibility; we must educate African American students as a means of liberating them from this difficult condition; we must help them build the self-esteem that will free them from the current despair and alienation that will otherwise manifest itself in anti-social activities, crime, and self-destruction.

Schools are a major key to this problem for the simple reason that success in school is the only institutionalized means available to African American youth for realizing pecuniary success and ultimately being rewarded by society. There are few if any choices for those who opt not to succeed in school. During the 1983-84 school year in the state of Michigan, for example, an aggregate of 22 percent of public school students entering the ninth grade failed to graduate from high school with their ninth grade cohorts. Among the 26,960 individual students who dropped out of that class statewide, the proportion is heavily skewed by race, as indicated in the tables that follow.

Data to Consider

Table 1
Dropout Rates by Racial-Ethnic Category
for the 1983-84 School Year in Michigan

Racial/Ethnic Group	Dropout Rate	Number of Dropouts
African American	11.7%	8,859
Hispanic	10.2%	721
Native American	6.3%	294
White	4.2%	16,964
Asian	3.7%	122

Table 2
Achievement in Mathematics: Trends

Ethnicity	1973	1978	1982	1986
9-year-olds				
Total	219.1	218.6	219.0	221.7
White	224.9	224.1	224.0	226.9
African American	190.0	192.4	194.9	201.6
Hispanic	202.1	202.9	204.0	205.4
13-year-olds				
Total	266.0	264.1	268.6	269.0
White	273.7	271.6	274.4	273.6
African American	227.7	229.6	240.4	249.2
Hispanic	238.8	238.0	252.4	254.3
17-year-olds				
Total	304.4	300.4	298.5	302.0
White	310.1	305.9	303.7	307.5
African American	269.8	268.4	271.8	278.6
Hispanic	277.2	276.3	276.7	283.1

Source "Achievement Scores in Mathematics by Age, Gender, and Ethnicity: 1973-86," *Science and Engineering Indicators--1989, 1989*, p. 190. Primary Source: National Assessment of Educational Progress, *The Mathematics Report Card: Are We Measuring Up?*, Report No. 17-M-01 (Princeton: Educational Testing Service, 1988).

Action Questions

Analyze Table 2 above on "Achievement in Mathematics." How do trends of whites compare with African Americans and Hispanics for 9-year-olds? What about 13-year-old and 17-year-old students? What group of students have made the greatest improvements over the years? How does your particular school compare with math achievement test scores in your own school? What could you do to improve the achievement test scores of your own school?

More Data

Table 3
Achievement in Science: Trends

Ethnicity	1970	1973	1977	1982	1986
9-year-olds					
Total	224.9	220.3	219.9	220.9	224.3
White	235.9	231.1	229.6	229.1	231.9
African American	178.7	176.5	174.9	187.1	196.2
Hispanic	na	na	191.9	189.0	199.4
13-year-olds					
Total	254.9	249.5	247.4	250.2	251.4
White	263.4	258.6	256.1	257.3	259.2
African American	214.9	205.3	208.1	217.2	221.6
Hispanic	na	na	213.4	225.5	226.1
17-year-olds					
Total	804.8	295.8	289.6	283.3	288.5
White	311.8	303.9	297.7	293.2	297.5
African American	257.8	250.4	240.3	234.8	252.8
Hispanic	na	na	262.3	248.7	259.3

Source: "Achievement Scores in Science by Age, Gender, and Ethnicity, 1970-96," *Science and Engineering Indicators—1989*, 1989, p. 186. Primary source: National Assessment of Educational Progress, *The Science Report Card: Elements of Risk and Recovery*, Report No. 17-S-01 (Princeton: Educational Testing Service, 1988).

Action Questions

Analyze Table 3 on "Achievement in Science." How do trends of whites compare with African Americans and Hispanics for 9-year-olds? What about 13-year-olds and 17-year-olds? What group of students have made the greatest gains in science over the years? How does your own school compare with these scores? What could be done to improve science achievement in your school?

The Drop Out Cycle and Violence

The dropout rates among African American, Hispanic, and Native American students in some Michigan school districts have been as high as 40 percent in recent years. A report from the Wayne State University College of Education indicates that school dropouts are prone to higher than average rates of unemployment, disproportionate representation in menial jobs, higher costs for health services, and long-term dependence on welfare. Such a relationship with low-paying and debilitating jobs, with the welfare system, and with health problems naturally eats away at the very core of one's existence; as such social problems plague African Americans disproportionately, the prospects looks bleak for future generations of African Americans until they can break out of this cycle of despair and alienation. (Wayne State University College of Education, 1987).

To fully address the difficulties of African American students, the schools will not only need to become more effective in teaching basic academic skills, but social skills must be developed as well. The tendency for African American students to resort to "Saturday Night Specials" as a problem-solving instrument must be vigorously challenged by the schools as well as other social institutions. All students must be taught a repertoire of socially acceptable and useful problem-solving skills. Otherwise, the major cause of death in this nation among young African Americans will continue to be young African Americans killing other young African Americans.

Effective schools need to be effective in the education of African

American students regardless of their economic and social background. The fostering of social and problem-solving skills must occur right along with the development of basic academic skills. Today's teachers must be prepared to deal with both social and educational issues and problems.

Action Questions

Consider a situation in which you as a teacher hear a rumor that one of the African American students in your school is carrying a gun and has threatened to shoot one of the other students. How do you handle this situation? How would you intervene? Are there strategies to prevent such things from happening again?

How is this related to the educational program? What can be done to reverse the dropout problems in your school?

Cultural Hegemony

White cultural hegemony is so powerful and has had such an impact upon African Americans that the predominant belief among African American youth is that white America feels that African Americans cannot learn. The sad part about it is that there are African American teachers and African American students themselves who feel they cannot learn, even though those same students can memorize the lyrics of top-ten records and tell you the name and the year various albums were recorded.

The constant devaluation of African Americans in this society can have long term effects upon the psyche, on one's emotional state, and on one's ability to learn. When we hear of African American students who are high achievers or who outscore whites on a standardized test, they are looked upon with suspicion. How can African American students do so well academically? Is there some hanky-panky going on with the test scores?

The movie *Standing Tall* and recent school statistics from Houston are examples. In the movie (a true one at that), Hispanics did extremely well academically on a standardized test, to the point where school administrators were in disbelief; they felt students had cheated and forced them to take the examination again. In Houston, white school officials were in disbelief and thought that African American educators and children were in some way cheating when the test scores at one elementary school far exceeded expectations. The sad part about these two stories is that both African

Americans and Hispanics were surprised, too. African American children can learn. Hispanic children can learn. It's as simple as that.

Exercise

You are a principal of a school that is predominantly African American and poor. Yet you have been successful in raising the students' academic achievement level to a point where they are out-scoring their white counterparts in the suburbs; they do better than whites on math and reading. Students from your school are among the top scoring in the state.

Yet you have failed to get the support or recognition from the administration; the superintendent has never visited the school, even though she has been in her position for four years. You feel that your school gets less of the available resources than other schools in the district. You have been criticized by other administrators and teachers in the system. They say that your teachers teach from the standardized test, that they teach students to pass what's on the test, even though no one has found that to be the case. They argue that this is not what education is about, that rote memorization thwarts creativity, and that too much emphasis is placed upon regimentation.

Continue to add to this scenario based upon your experience.

Action Questions

As an administrator, how would you respond to such criticism? As a teacher, how would you respond?

More specifically, if teachers were teaching from standardized tests, how would you respond to this charge? How would you respond to the charge that rote memorization thwarts creativity? What other schools can you name where African American or Hispanic students are excelling academically? What do you think contributes to the school's success?

How do you go about getting the recognition and support your school needs to be even better at what it already does successfully? What are other questions you should ask regarding this scenario?

Another Exercise

Every month school superintendent Anderson meets with the principals of the schools in the district. You are the principal of a predominantly African American elementary school. For several months, Mr. Jackson, the principal of the predominantly African American high school has raised the issue of an all African American male high school—since African American females are doing much better academically than males, he is pushing for a segregated school of African American males.

Mr. Jackson feels that the African American male students need discipline and strong male models in order for them to reverse the trend of academic failure. In his view, schools as they are presently constituted were not fulfilling the needs of African American male students. In your own school, African American males have done poorly academically. On the one hand, Mr. Jackson makes sense, but you want to test this idea out with your staff. At the next staff meeting, you raise the issue of a separate school for African American males. You want teachers to answer the following questions.

Action Questions

Pretend that you are teachers at this school meeting. In what ways will a separate school have the potential of increasing the academic performance of African American males? In what ways will it not increase the performance of African American male students?

What would make teaching better in an all male African American school? In what ways would it be worse? Is the separation by gender the answer, or is it the failure of teachers to teach, or something else?

In what ways is an all African American male school a move back to segregated schools?

Is such an educational plan against the law? Should we be concerned about the law, about desegregated schools, or should we only be concerned about what might work educationally? What are other questions that should be asked?

Teacher Expectations

Contemporary educational literature is replete with the discussion of teaching methods—a myriad of ideas to improve instruction and foster greater student achievement. The effectiveness of many of these methodologies has been amply demonstrated in at last some school settings, and it is likely that teachers in other schools can and do find success in applying such new ideas. But before one rushes to try new procedures, some basic questions must be addressed.

Perhaps most basic is the question of whose interests are to be served? Is the teacher, as well as the creator of the new methodology, seeking a way of making the teaching job easier, or of profiting from the attendant publicity and success? Or is there a genuine desire to serve the students, to increase the expectation for success, to reverse some of the debilitating patterns that come with failure in school?

The evidence is mounting that attitude and expectation on the part of the teacher is a paramount factor in student achievement. Asa Hilliard has stated that since the most important variable is the attitude of the teacher, then the specific teaching method will seldom make that much of a difference. Any viable instructional method will succeed if the teacher exhibits an positive attitude of expectation towards the students that signals that they will succeed (Hilliard, 1987).

If, on the other hand, the teacher does not appear committed to the class, or exhibits an attitude of contempt for any or all of the students, then no matter what teaching method is employed, there will be no universal success.

Teacher attitude and expectation is the key. If the teacher has high expectations for all students, and clearly and openly communicates that fact to the class, that person's teaching will reap success whatever specific method is used.

Action Questions

We ask that you think about this notion of attitude and expectation. Is it more important than instructional methodology? Or is it, in and of itself, an instructional method? Think about your own educational experiences, and list as many different teaching methods as you can. Do you believe Hilliard's contention that any and all of these methods will work, as long as they are accompanied by an attitude which conveys an expectation of success?

If you agree, then think about how you and other teachers can implement such strategies. If you disagree, then consider what kinds of situations or teaching methods you feel will fail, even with a positive attitude, and what methods you think will succeed, even without such expectations of success.

Professional Development

If schools are to play a leading role in fostering the social and academic success of all students, then it is clear that we are asking teachers to shoulder some significant new responsibilities along with the school principal and other educational leaders. If teachers are to create and implement new classroom strategies, and exhibit attitudes and expectations that are geared to encourage and actualize success on the part of all students, then there will need to be a solid program of professional development in place to assist and guide all faculty.

All teachers can profit from additional college and university instruction, from workshops, and from other inservice opportunities, since all such activities offer new ideas and an opportunity to consider different educational strategies and approaches. But the key to professional development must occur at the school site, through opportunities to talk with other members of the teaching staff, to exchange effective teaching procedures, and to build a climate that fosters the positive attitude and expectations that must be communicated and passed along to the students.

Perhaps the best model for such dialogue comes in the form of the "quality circles" which have evolved from the industrial model in both the United States and Japan. Through the use of quality circle discussions and action research paradigms, the teaching staff at all schools can develop a climate of success, an atmosphere that can then be passed along to the students (Bryant, 1988).

Teachers individually have considerable technical skills to offer each other, and the personal experiences of each teacher can be productive in improving the performance of one's colleagues. Obviously, more experienced teachers may have more proven practices to share with their colleagues, while newer teachers may bring some different ideas and some renewed vigor to the setting. Such collegial interaction will require some form of released time for all members of the staff, a portion of which must be in common so that quality circle groups can gather and exchange ideas. The pairing of teachers to observe each other in their classrooms and to meet to discuss reactions can also be of great value in breaking down the traditional isolation of each teacher working solo in his or her private classroom.

Teacher professional development should not be limited to time spent with other teachers. Teachers should also interact with administrators, and should spend some of their time observing and standing in for administrators to gain an appreciation of the challenges and problems principals and other school leaders have to address. In reverse, principals and other administrators should step into the classroom often, do a bit of teaching, and interact with their teaching staffs about the educational strategies that will best improve student performance.

Action Questions

Think about what kind of professional development program would work best in your school. Have you tried a quality circle approach among your teaching staff? Do you have adequate time to get together with colleagues, to exchange ideas and strategies? Do you take turns observing each other and seeking improvement in your instruction?

What would it take to initiate such efforts in your school? What other professional development ideas do you have? How would you go about freeing up an hour and a half a week for teachers to meet on school time?

Clarifying Philosophy

Often it's important, as a part of both preservice and inservice training, to get teachers involved in value clarification regarding their philosophy about teaching. In doing so, administrators can then begin not only to identify and surface the differences that might exist within their teaching staff, but can use such differences to set the framework for substantive educational discussion.

Too often, we make assumptions about our peers and subordinates and their educational philosophy. Too often, there is a discrepancy between one's educational philosophy and one's teaching behavior; a person, although saying great things about teaching, may act contrary to those stated beliefs. Such discrepancies between teaching and professed beliefs should be discussed. In other instances, teachers have not thought much at all about their teaching philosophy, even though their philosophy is expressed in their relations to students. Following is an exercise to get teachers thinking about their educational philosophy.

An Exercise

This exercise requires a large room with chairs arranged in circles in each of the four corners of the room. On each wall on large sheets of newsprint are listed these possible answers—"Strongly Agree" (north wall), "Agree" (west wall), "Disagree" (east wall), and "Strongly Disagree" (south wall).

Each teacher is given a copy of a questionnaire. This questionnaire consists of questions to be answered by the four posted responses. All participants are asked initially to stand in the center of the room; as the facilitator reads each question, each teacher is to mark the appropriate response on their questionnaire, and then physically place themselves under the sheet posted on the wall that corresponds to the answer they marked on the questionnaire.

As they stand in these groups, they are to spend three to four minutes discussing why they chose their particular answer. Then they are asked to return to the center of the room. Another question is read, and the process repeats itself until all the questions have been read and answered.

As participants position themselves under the sheets on the wall that reflect their answers, the facilitator is to use his or her questionnaire to keep track of the distribution on each question. The questions with equal distributions or loadings become candidates to be picked as the basis of heterogeneous groups for more substantive discussion.

After the facilitator selects a question with equal loadings, participants are asked once again to place their bodies according to how they answered the question before. Then the facilitator puts together several mixed groups of equal numbers of people reflecting the response categories.

The questions for the questionnaire are as follows:

◆ African American students cannot be taught the

same way as whites because they require a lot more discipline and control.

◆ Separateness of the races is as important as integration and should be cherished.

◆ Students should always be given a choice in deciding curriculum issues.

◆ Students should be involved in the evaluation of teacher performance and such evaluations should be considered in the meritorious promotion and incremental salary increases.

◆ There is a positive relationship between teachers' salaries and the academic achievement of their students.

◆ There is no relationship between the amount of money spend per student and academic achievement.

◆ The principal is the most important educator in motivating teachers and students, and setting an atmosphere for high motivation and achievement.

◆ Teacher attitude is more important for student achievement than any one teaching method.

◆ The lack of parental educational support of their children is the main reason why students fail to achieve.

◆ Students can learn and do well on standardized achievement tests regardless of their social class backgrounds.

◆ The higher the school expenditure for students, the higher the student motivation for academic achievement.

◆ All teachers from K-12th grade should teach reading, regardless of their assigned subject matter.

◆ All teachers should be counselors and substitute parents to help students, based upon their needs, in order that students may be successful academically.

◆ Structure and clear expectations, rather than affective education, are strategies for the effective teaching of African American students.

Finally, the facilitator, depending upon how large the group, selects individuals in pairs from each wall or distribution to make up heterogeneous groupings for discussion. Each heterogeneous group is to find a space in one of the corners and begin its discussion.

The task is to influence, and even to get someone else to change their educational philosophy. This continues for about twenty minutes, at which point participants evaluate the exercise and report if there have been changes in their attitudes or if they have gained new philosophical insights.

Examples of Building Off Student Strengths

A significant part of creating an effective school is the provision of an opportunity for students to share, have pride in, and build upon their non-academic talents. While there is no clear line between student abilities that are part of the regular academic program, and those that are more regularly practiced outside the school, the idea here is to make use of student talents which might otherwise go unnoticed in school.

For example, in one school the principal holds weekly school-wide assemblies in which he presents awards for outstanding achievement by students in their school academic activities, as well as in such other categories as polite behavior, thoughtfulness, and other positive traits which have been observed. In addition, this particular principal will give a talk about some positive aspect of the school in general as a means of getting all of the students to take greater pride in their school.

As part of such programs, individual students are encouraged to read poems they have written, play musical instruments, and present skits and other cooperative activities. Overall, this principal is building upon the strengths of the students and allowing them to share and demonstrate their talents, thereby creating a positive image not only of the performers, but of the school in general.

Another principal has the high school band drive through the school neighborhood, made up largely of poor housing projects, on a flatbed truck, playing music for the neighborhood. In this way, he has been able to improve public relations for the school, and create a sense that the school belongs to the community.

This latter principal has also arranged for the school's commencement exercises to be broadcast on local radio, so that those members of the community unable to attend could listen to the proceedings. Using community access television would be another possible technique.

Such procedures for expanding the image of the school

in a positive manner go a long way towards creating a base of community support, particularly when it comes time to seek an increase in funding through a vote on local millage.

Action Questions

All teachers and principals should explore together ways in which they can improve the school climate by capitalizing on the talents and abilities of the school children in both academic and non-academic areas. What things can you do to allow students to showcase their talents, to improve their individual self-esteem, and to contribute to a more positive school atmosphere?

What forces currently either help or hinder the involvement of students in your school? What things could be done to reach out to your community and build a more cooperative attitude toward the school?

Parental Involvement

Teachers and school managers need all the help they can get in tackling the problems involved in fostering positive educational experiences for all students. Schools must reach out to parents and children well before the normal school-entering age. Public schools should provide classes in parenting for members of the school community. School aides should be available to go to the homes of young children and work with the parents in development of early skills. Schools should establish links for support and assistance with day care and other early childhood programs in the community.

The schools can also develop procedures to work with parents of their school-age students. Courses in parenting, both for parents in the community and for students as future parents, could become a part of the school program. The possibilities for cooperation between social service, public health, and educational agencies to foster a better climate for the emotional and academic success of all children are many, and it is time that schools explored a leadership role in this area.

Scenario

Consider, for example, that you are an administrator in

an elementary school with a high African American enroll-
ment. Your students are next to last in achievement on
district reading and mathematics scores.

You also notice that a high percentage of the children
in your school now are the sons and daughters of students
who were there little more than a decade ago; you have
tried to establish rapport with these young parents, but
with little if any success. You can see a community pattern
that is working against success in school, and therefore in
life in general.

Action Questions

What can you as a school administrator do? Can you
establish some cooperative arrangements with local health
or welfare offices? Can you require young parents to get
more involved in school conferences about their children?

What kind of support will you need from your school
district and other authorities to develop such cooperative
programs? What are the potential advantages and disadvantages for your school?

Community Involvement

The general lack of involvement in school affairs on the part of parents
and the community at large, particularly in poor and minority neighborhoods, is nothing new to American education. Indeed, many educators have
been quite happy with this arrangement, since it has usually meant that
there was no one questioning or interfering with the school program. In
reality, however, it also means that there is no one in the home or the
neighborhood of the students providing emotional or moral support for that
school program.

If we are to foster universal success in our schools, we must find ways
to involve the parents and the community, to encourage them to become
partners to the success of this desired teaching and learning proess. There
are no magical answers, but we as educators must continue to seek ways to
foster this sort of involvement. As consumers of education, parents need to
be involved so that they can more effectively help their children. There are
many potential strategies, of which the following are but a few examples.

Examples

Some schools have succeeded in developing a contract with each parent and child concerning academic goals for the school year. The contract commits the parents to helping their child with homework, making sure that assignments are completed, and that work is done neatly and correctly. The parents must become integrally involved with the school and the teacher in order to know how to help students proceed in that direction.

Other schools have set aside a special room, with comfortable and modern furniture, that creates a welcoming atmosphere. Such a lounge is open to parents during school hours as a place to visit, to meet with teachers and the principal, to arrange for observations of classrooms, and to discuss school issues. Such rooms can be equipped with a few telephones, and used as places for involved parents to call other parents and invite them to also get involved.

Yet other schools have established special events, such as a monthly breakfast for parents at the school, to which other members of the community, such as clergy, representatives of the Chamber of Commerce, school board members, the chief of police, and the local media are also invited. Such meetings can provide opportunities for the media to report favorably about school activities, and various segments of the community can be encouraged to provide additional support for the school.

Action Questions

You are invited to think about such things creatively. What other ways are there to effectively involve the parents and the community in support of your educational program?

How can you effectively use parents in the school? What kinds of contracts can you devise that will draw parents in and encourage them to help and support the work of their children? What roles can others in the community, such as clergy, business people, the police, and the politicians play?

As you come up with novel ideas, share them with other educators and see what you can put into effective practice.

Expectation is the Goal

Remember that the goal of all such efforts is to create a climate in your school, and in each classroom in that school, that exudes an attitude of success, in which there is the clear expectation that all children will achieve. Whatever gimmicks you may devise in that direction, whatever groups you get involved, and whatever professional development programs are used, all such things should contribute to the expectation that the children will learn, will achieve, and will succeed.

Nothing should get in the way of that ultimate goal.

Notes

Criteria III:
The Atmosphere

The third criteria offered by Edmonds is that effective schools must provide an atmosphere which is orderly without being rigid. Students cannot learn unless there is discipline in the classroom; nor can teachers teach in an undisciplined situation. Discipline is an important ingredient for both teaching and learning, yet is not something that is readily present in contemporary American schools. It must be achieved initially through cooperation between teachers and administrators in developing a plan which will then assure cooperation from students in implementing proper discipline.

Appropriate discipline ranges from the simple level of respect between teachers and students that will allow instruction and learning to occur in every classroom to the assurance of a school atmosphere that is free of drug dependence, weapons, and other threats to individual safety.

It is a must that schools create and maintain organizational norms that are safe for teachers and students alike.

Clean and Safe Buildings

It is obvious that school buildings that are clean and safe will foster a far better climate for learning that those that are not. Clean buildings and classrooms make a fundamental statement about the teachers and students who work within them; they establish a climate for learning and achievement. Clean schools also speak to the issue of student health, and create an atmosphere that encourages attention to the health and welfare of the students.

The issue of safety—of a school situation in which neither teachers nor students must fear physical abuse or worry about threats to life or limb—is also of obvious importance. One cannot expect attention to be given to teaching and learning if either teachers or students are in constant fear.

A Scenario

Think about the implications of unsafe schools. Pretend, for a moment, that you teach in a high school in a rough neighborhood. Teachers' cars have been stolen from the school parking lot; tires have been slashed. Angry parents have stormed the school, and teachers have been threatened with bodily harm. Papers and trash are constantly in the hallways.

You can fill in other details of this situation, all of which work against effective education.

Action Questions

How would you react to this scenario? What should be done to make such a school safe and clean? What effective strategies or tactics are you familiar with? What would you do to turn such a school into an effective learning environment?

Are there agencies or individuals outside of the school itself on which you could call for help? To what degree is this a community problem, or a political problem, as well as an educational problem?

Group and Organizational Norms

In situations where schools are unsafe and unclean, one of the key problems is the operationalization of negative group norms. Once a community has given up on its school, and the patterns of behavior involve the trashing of the school facility and the frequency of physical abuse, weapons, drugs, and other indicators of anti-social behavior, it is very difficult to reverse such trends.

Social scientists have documented time and time again the powerful nature of social norms. Once in place, such patterns tend to determine what is and is not acceptable behavior. In fact, studies have shown that social norms can be so powerful that they destroy one's reality and lead to mental illness.

Group norms in schools can, in a very broad sense, be termed either positive or negative. Our concern here is with negative norms—norms that foster patterns of deviant behavior, of vandalism to school property, of trashing of halls and classrooms, of lack of interest in the educational program, and of acts of physical abuse. Such norms create an atmosphere for students that discourages learning, even to the degree that students who do wish to learn are afraid to do so for fear of reprisal from their peers. Such norms also encourage anti-social behavior, ranging from skipping classes, smoking on school property, and vandalism, on to a wide range of clearly criminal behavior.

Such negative school norms also affect teachers in many ways, leading to discouragement, despair, burnout, fear, and ultimately to situations in which the teachers simply give up on any efforts to accomplish their educational goals.

A Scenario

We ask that you think about such school situations. For example, consider Richard, who is a transfer student from an all-African American school to an integrated school. As the new kid in school, he gets into a fight with another African American student, and he is then not accepted by yet other African American students at his new school.

Although he had not been a high achieving student previously, he decides that at the new school he will do his best in class. One day in class he raises his hand to answer one of the teacher's questions, and he notices that the other African American students are frowning at him with disapproval. They are putting pressure on him to not succeed in class, because his success would violate their group norms.

Action Questions

What does Richard do? Will he give in to this pressure or not?

Have you ever experienced an educational situation like this? How did you handle it, or how would you handle it? What would you say to Richard, and to the other students?

Are there ways in which you can alter such group norms, and substitute positive expectations where the norms are now negative?

Classroom Discipline

The lack of academic achievement in many American schools is closely correlated with poor classroom discipline. Without effective discipline, very little learning can take place. Teachers are not able to teach effectively, and students are unable to give necessary attention to the subject matter at hand. As such problems have worsened in many schools, both administrators and teachers have struggled to identify ways to restore and maintain effective discipline.

While it is seldom admitted, rebellious high school students are often a threat to the personal security of both teachers and administrators. Such students make us feel inadequate when they fail to respond to our direction. They make us truly fearful in those most serious of situations where physical abuse and weapons are involved. Often teachers and administrators conclude that they have few if any options available for effective control of students. In too many instances they simply give up and give in to the situation.

Contemporary educational literature suggests, however, that most educational situations can be controlled with proven approaches to classroom discipline. What is required is a systematic and consistent plan of action, developed cooperatively by the teachers and administrators and even in concert with the students, and then pursued with rigor.

Some experts in this field suggest that such a plan should include individual and group rewards for specific academic accomplishments, as well as consistent procedures for the removal of trouble-making students from the classroom in order to maintain a climate for effective teaching and learning (Cantor, 1987).

Other experts suggest that instead of a traditional reward-and-punishment approach, teachers and school managers should develop a school atmosphere that emphasizes student responsibility and encourages the learning of democratic social skills that will be needed in adulthood (Gathercoal, 1991).

A Senario

Think about specific problems of student discipline. Imagine that you are lecturing to a class, and three of your students—Bill, Greg, and Tom—are passing notes and whispering loudly. You continue your lecture, but at the same time write their names on the blackboard, thus indicating that you are aware of their behavior and that it is time for them to shape up. Greg ceases his role in the disruption, but Bill and Tom continue whispering, and you place a check next to their names. Each such check will result in some form of disciplinary action later.

Three checks by a name means a phone call to the student's parents or a trip to the principal's office for disciplinary purposes. Tom is disrupting the class, and you ask him to leave. He refuses. You give the class a reading assignment, then walk over to your desk, unlock the bottom drawer, and pull out your AT&T cordless telephone. You look up the phone number of Tom's parents, step just outside the classroom door and call his parents. Tom's mother answers the phone and you identify yourself as being Mrs. Rogers, Tom's teacher and you talk to her about Tom's behavior. The parent agrees to talk with her son. You step back into the class and call Tom to the phone. Three minutes later Tom hands the phone to you and takes off to the principal's office. You thank Tom's mother for her help. You then call the assistant principal's office and let Johnson know that Tom is supposed to report there and for what reasons. You also suggest some punishment for Tom. You know that if the phone call failed to have an impact upon Tom's behavior, then you would have called the principal's office directly and had someone come to physically take Tom from the room. (Ideas from Cantor, 1987.)

Action Questions

How might the telephone be used differently? Can a cordless telephone be used realistically in the classroom? Are you familiar with such school discipline proce-

dures, or with other routines which have proven successful? If you were involved in such a system, what do you feel
should be the result of writing a student's name on the
board, or placing a check after it? What kinds of punishment are effective? How can teachers and administrators
work together to establish such procedures for a school?

Experts suggest that the telephone should only be used sparingly, and
it's a signal to students that you will call their parents immediately. After
you have done this a few times, there will be less need to use the phone—
probably none at all. Eventually you can take your cordless phone back
home with you. If you don't have access to a phone, then work it out with
the teacher next door to give you some assistance in handling a difficult
student.

Action Questions

In addition to disciplinary measures that punish unac-
ceptable behavior, are there ways to develop a system of
rewards for good behavior? If everyone gets their assignments in on time, some teachers will allow a few minutes of
informal talking or music at the end of the period. Other
teachers will allow a pizza party or some other such event
once in a while, in the belief that such rewards will help
form and encourage positive group norms in the classroom.

Can you think of other ways to reward students for
both individual and group behavior that fosters learning
and achievement? Have you attempted approaches like
the ones described above? How well did they work?

What kind of overall discipline plan or approach would
work best in your school? Do you have such a plan in place?
If not, what sort of assistance do you need to develop and
implement such a plan?

Discipline Plans

We do not suggest that there is any one right way to foster discipline in
a school setting. But whatever method is employed, it should be consistent.
Some of the procedures described above as examples work well in some
settings, but might not work in others. Lack of consistency often times leads

to confusion and ambiguity, and thus any disciplinary option may become ineffective.

Another key rule to follow is that punishment should be fair; it should be given not out of malice, but with an intent to help the student become more responsible. The key point is that effective discipline must be maintained in all schools and all classrooms if learning is to take place. Thus, all teachers and administrators are challenged to work together to define the problems in their schools and to develop a plan that they can implement cooperatively, consistently, and effectively.

Notes

Notes

Criteria IV:
Basic Skills

The fourth criteria for effective schools suggested by Edmonds involves pupil acquisition of basic skills. He suggests that this goal must take precedence over all other school activities, and that energy and resources should be diverted from any and all other business of the school to assure that all pupils acquire basic academic skills that will serve as the foundation for their ongoing education and success in their adult lives.

To assure an effective educational program for all students, what is called for is a mobilization of all teachers and all available human and material resources, regardless of grade level or specialization, to first teach basic study skills and the rudiments of reading, writing, and mathematics to all students.

In addition to such a focus by all regular teachers, utilization of teacher aides and volunteers in the classroom can provide important support to teachers in effectively reaching all students. One study of effective schools, however, found that high-achieving schools were characterized by limited non-instructional use of teacher aides; this suggests that the regular teachers were handling basic instruction in those classrooms (Madden, 1976). This does not mean, on the other hand, that there are not effective ways to use aides and volunteers in support of such basic instruction.

In addition to the deployment of personnel committed to instruction in basic skills, many other strategies can and must be used as well. Attention to individual student needs can be addressed through cross-age teaching, in which high school youth tutor elementary students, for example.

Given the power, accessibility, and potential of the computer as an educational tool, as well as the allure it has for many students, classroom computers should also be utilized for instruction in basic skills where possible.

Study Skills

In the *A Nation at Risk* report, it was clearly articulated that students in the United States are not mastering academic skills at a wholly desirable level. Reading and writing difficulties are reaching epidemic proportions in many of our schools. Traditionally, such skills have been left to specialists among our teaching force, but it would appear that such skills are too basic and too important to be handled only by a few teachers.

Rather, it is time to develop coordinated instructional programs in our schools. Every teacher should have a role in fostering effective reading and writing skills, regardless of specific instructional specialization. Such a coordinated approach would call upon each teacher to use some basic reading and writing skills in the presentation of his or her subject matter, and to require all students to practice and demonstrate mastery of such skills in every class.

While such coordinated approaches would vary depending upon the grade levels and subjects being taught, there are a myriad of techniques that could be employed, ranging from attention to topic sentences within the instructional textbook being used (see description later in this section of a technique used at the University of Michigan) to brief writing assignments summarizing daily class presentations on the subject at hand.

In essence, every teacher becomes an instructor in the essential elements of reading and writing. Every teacher takes some responsibility for assigning reading and writing activities that involve facility with the common elements of grammar, spelling, and other communications skills. All teachers should have received some introductory training in these essentials, and should feel a commitment to assisting with a coordinated program that will assure that students at all levels of their education develop, retain, and enhance such basic academic abilities.

Action Questions

All educators should consider how such a coordinated approach can best be designed and implemented. Obviously some commitment of instructional time would be necessary, but not to such an extent that it would vitiate other academic and instructional goals.

What are the problems involved in assuring that basic academic skills are required and used in every classroom? What are the forces afoot in our schools that would tend to preclude such a coordinated instructional effort?

What role should administrators, and particularly school principals, play in developing such a program? What needs to be done to get such a commitment from all teachers?

Note-Taking

Why is note-taking so important? Why should such skills be taught in schools? Note-taking is important because it involves developing the memory capacity to attend, store, and manipulate information selected from a lecture (Kiewra *et al*, 1987). It is a process of transcribing ideas previously presented. It is a multifaceted set of skills involving comprehension, cognitive demands, and discourse.

Students without note-taking skills only capture a small part of lectures or presentations. Most research supports comprehensive note-taking and the systematic review of those notes as being clearly associated with academic achievement (Kiewra, 1984; Kiewra, 1985a; Kiewra and Benton, 1988).

Note-taking allows the note-taker to gather meaningful and complex propositions, which are then captured and expressed by clauses or sentences that convey a single idea. This process fosters and enhances the ability to combine complex propositions so that meaningful connections can be made between successive sentences, resulting in an articulate theme or topic of discourse.

Note-taking has two basic functions: 1) it has an encoding function in which the lecture material is transformed into a more useful and meaningful form to help the learner remember; and 2) it has an external storage function through which students are able to keep and review the material later.

Both functions are important. Note-taking without review is not as effective for academic success; note-taking with immediate review proves to be the most successful. Note-taking also serves as a basis for developing reading comprehension and solid study habits.

An Example

For example, in a study method developed at the University of Michigan, students are encouraged to: 1) read the topic sentences of each paragraph in the chapter; 2) read the summary or conclusion carefully; 3) outline the chapter of the book by turning each topic sentence of each paragraph into a question; 4) then read the material in order to answer the question, thereby helping students pick out the important points of the paragraph; and, finally, 4) immediately review the notes.

Students who review such notes once a week typically do much better on mid-semester and final examinations.

Action Questions

How would you experiment with note-taking and developing study skills in your class? How can you get other teachers to teach note-taking in their classes, regardless of subject matter? How does note-taking relate to writing?

What are the barriers against teaching note-taking? What are the facilitating forces in the school that would support note-taking?

Possible Interventions

Traditionally, in American education, the same organizational structure has been used in all schools, with the goal of educating all children. Ironically, this has continued even though research into learning tells us that not all children learn best in the same ways.

As we face the crisis of educating increasing numbers of minority and disadvantaged students, it is necessary for us to create some new instructional strategies—some educational interventions that will allow schools, and the students and faculty within them, to gain control of the educational process. Such new approaches will improve the student-teacher relationship, and thereby enhance the overall school atmosphere.

One such intervention strategy is the three-year cycle, in which students will remain with the same teacher through three consecutive grades. Together they proceed through three years of curriculum, advancing together educationally. The primary disadvantage of the three-year cycle is that students will experience fewer teachers as adult models, and thus fewer educational points of view. However, this may be outweighed by the advantage that comes with students and teachers developing strong educational bonds over a long period of time. Such a bonding and support system is particularly important for students coming from unsettled homes and neighborhood situations, where they need some stability and consistency in their lives.

By involving teachers in this three-year cycle, the school fosters a learning environment in which one can get to know one's students and build a long-standing relationship with them. This approach also enhances teacher accountability, since teachers who work with the same student over a longer period are clearly more directly responsible for seeing that each of those students acquires the necessary basic skills. No longer can the teacher readily place the blame on some other teacher who had the student the year before. Over a three-year period, the teacher has time to work with each student and to assure that skills and abilities are properly developed.

As appropriate to the needs of the students and the school system, this three-year cycle can be put in place at all grade levels. In elementary schools, for example, teachers could work with the same class of students in first-second-and-third grade or fourth-fifth-and-sixth grade groupings, as well as other possible combinations. At the secondary level, for example, it could be implemented by having students remain with the same set of teachers for their various subject matter fields over the three years of junior or senior high school

Obviously, such a radical restructuring of school organization would raise some controversy.

A Scenario

Consider the following possible discussions as a high school principal calls his teachers together after they have served as the core teachers for the same group of students over a three-year period. As he closes the door to his office, the principal states: "I thought it would be good for us to evaluate the past three years together, to review the experience in terms of highs and lows. I want to know what you think."

The teachers sat and stared at one another for a minute, until the silence was broken by the science teacher, a woman who said: "Well, I think this new three-year organizational structure accomplished what it was supposed to. Teaching students this way enabled me to build a more intense relationship with each student, and gave me a greater sense of control over the classroom. I really got to know the students intimately—they were no longer just faces and names, I got to know their problems and concerns."

"Yeah," interrupted the English teacher, "I feel I have no other experience to compare with this. I felt under pressure to perform. I had to spend a lot of time preparing lessons to keep up with the various students. If a student couldn't write a sentence in the tenth grade three years ago, I knew that if that was still true by the twelfth grade that I would be to blame."

"But isn't that the way it should be," chimed in the history teacher. "We have to make ourselves more accountable. I feel we did a better job teaching because we were able to use our stronger relationships with these kids to influence them as they matured over the three years."

"Yes," said the mathematics teacher, a young man who had been peering out of the office window until now. "We may have improved the school's atmosphere, but it seems to me that the students should have been exposed to a greater variety of teachers, with different teaching abilities and values. And what about those situations where a particular student and teacher don't hit it off well. It's not fair to either of us to be together for three years."

"But that's no different than it has always been," stated the music teacher. "Haven't we always just tolerated some students, knowing that we will be rid of them in a year at most. That way we just pass our problems on to one another. In this three-year system we have to take responsibility for each student, and find ways in which we can get along and teach them and help them adjust to school."

"I agree," said the English teacher. "Once I knew that I was going to have Bill Williams in class for three years, I found ways to relate to him, and to help him gain the basic skills that had previously eluded him. I knew there would be no other teacher to pass him on to at the end of the year. In the traditional system I wouldn't have been called upon to make that kind of effort."

"There is so much pain and confusion that students experience these days," explained the Spanish teacher. "Lots of these students come from violent homes, and that violence is reinforced by what they experience in their neighborhoods and see on television. Students need to have some stable relationships in their lives, with adults on whom they can count. They need to be firmly grounded. I feel the three-year cycle has provided this opportunity for students to build positive relationships with us. This does not guarantee that each student will have had a positive relationship with each one of us, but the opportunity existed for good relationships to develop. Having positive relationships with adults is very important to students at this point in their lives."

"Well," said the mathematics teacher, "I'm not saying that I didn't enjoy this experience, but I'm not sure it would be a model for all schools to follow. Perhaps after we have improved the atmosphere of the school this way, we can return to the traditional structure."

Action Questions

This is a conversation that you are encouraged to continue with your own educational colleagues.

As a teacher or school administrator, how do you feel about the prospects of a three-year cycle in your school? Do you identify with the comments of any of the specific teachers in this scenario? Are there other issues that were not raised in this brief discussion?

What resistance would be encountered in your school system if this were seriously proposed? How would you go about implementing such a plan? What kinds of support would you need?

Cross-Age Teaching

Given the degree to which illiteracy in both language and mathematics has been identified as a national problem, and the fact that such skills are essential if individuals are to lead a productive and rewarding life in today's increasingly technological society, it seems only natural that we should deploy all available educational resources to eliminate such illiteracy. Not only should every teacher, regardless of subject or grade level, incorporate some reading and writing instruction into their classroom program, but they should also make use of our more advanced, older, and mature students to serve as tutors for younger students.

There are many school systems in which particularly able and interested high school student have been given an opportunity to help teach younger students, but such programs have seldom if ever truly plumbed the available resources of cross-age instruction. Consider that, at least potentially, all high school students—even those whose reading and mathematics skills are not up to grade level—will possess enough skills to offer elementary children some basic tutoring.

As teachers, we know that it takes time and energy to prepare for a lesson, to effectively master the necessary material. If this responsibility is placed, even briefly, on high school students, it will be an additional motivation for them to improve their own basic skills in order to pass those skills on to younger children.

The provision of tutoring assignments to high school students may also help give them some status and perhaps long-overdue recognition, as well as help convince them that they do have something to offer to other people. For the elementary school students involved in this relationship, cross-age tutoring will provide them with some individualized instruction, and with an older friend who can talk with them and help them along in school.

You are encouraged to consider a variety of ways to broaden the instructional program in basic skills, and to make cross-age tutoring available to both older and younger students.

A Scenario

Consider a situation in which you are a high school teacher and you notice that many of the students in your class are reading at only the third grade level. At a district-wide staff meeting, you learn from conversation with an elementary teacher that reading instruction in the lower grades is becoming more and more of a problem, because there is not time to give all students individual attention.

Since your two schools are not far apart geographically, you suggest that maybe some of your high school students who need to give more attention to their own reading skills might work individually with elementary students. Since you have computers in your school, you could assign high school students who are poor readers to create and write stories for elementary school children. These stories could be prepared in an attractive manner using laser printers, graphics, and pictures. Then the high school students could read their stories to the class, or have them read by the elementary school students.

Action Questions

How would you go about setting up such a program? Is this a good way for your high school students to use a free period in their school day? Are they really up to such an assignment? What kinds of benefits can you expect?

What sort of resistance will you encounter? What support do you need from your administration and from other teachers?

Computers

The computer age is apparently here to stay. The power and value of the computer is already apparent in many aspects of our everyday lives. It is a common tool in most areas of employment. Although the use of computers has at times been controversial in education, it is something that we all need to explore. The computer as a teaching tool has been criticized because of the lack of human contact, and because of fatigue and other physical effects associated with lengthy computer use.

On the positive side, however, is the fact that computers make information more accessible for learning, which in turn can support the instructional activities of the teacher. With the computer as a tool, one can focus more on teaching students how to learn, rather than just memorizing facts.

Computer instruction is already taking place at many levels of our educational system, and more is surely in the future. The power of the computer will undoubtedly become one of the pervasive teaching and learning technologies of the future.

One of the most exciting success stories of computer instruction is in the Biology 112 course at the University of Michigan. In a period of just three years of intensified computer instruction, African American students in that course—a group that has traditionally done very poorly on biology examinations—have improved from mean scores of 48.0 to 80.3, while the overall class mean for white students continued to be 81.2 (Kleinsmith, 1987). In another year or two, there will probably be no difference between the performance of African American and white students in that course.

This kind of significant educational improvement is not a fluke, but rather demonstrates the power of this new instructional technology. The use of that technology, and the instructional games that are part of it, have had a strong attraction for the African American students in that course. This computer instruction program is not only used to efficiently teach biology, but it is used to teach other subjects as well.

In fact, more often than not these days, it is the teacher rather than the students who is intimidated by computers. All of our children, through the power of television and the attractions of video arcades, have come into contact with at least some of the offshoots of computer technology. It is an exciting new culture, and one that appeals to nearly all children, whatever their social or cultural background. Given this natural appeal, it is only logical for teachers and schools to build upon it as another way of reaching those children who are otherwise difficult to educate.

The computer lends itself to many exciting educational strategies. Not only can it be used to enhance and individualize classroom instruction, but in the future, when it is more prevalent, it can also be used for conferencing among students on both school and non-school topics, including cooperation on homework assignments and building of life-long interests. Such computer networking has already been demonstrated to be a good way to involve other people from the community in the education and enlightenment of children. In many ways, it is like setting up a computer hot line for students, teachers, parents, and others in the community to assist with school work and to encourage interests of many kinds.

A Scenario

Consider, for instance, that in your school district it is likely that many of your students have computers at home, or at least have access to a family microcomputer. You know that in many cases they already spend a lot of free time playing computer games. You have also noticed a clear correlation between those students involved in such computer activities and their success in school.

Action Questions

What would you make of this scenario? Are there ways in which you can get someone to help you develop some educational games that will be attractive to these students, and serve to focus their computer time on academic topics?

What other questions need to be addressed in this area? How would you go about getting support for computer instruction in your classroom? Are computers useful and relevant to all subject areas in school, to all grade levels?

Would other teachers in your school wish to use computers in their classes?

Is there a budget for such activities? What does your administration think of computer instruction? Do you know of schools with successful programs of computer use? Do you know of computer conferencing and hot lines in your area? If so, how might they be relevant to your educational work with students?

Homework

While some students have little difficulty accomplishing homework assignments, others have a great deal of difficulty. The question is, how can the resources of some students be used to help others?

One possibility is for the teacher to form telephone hot line homework teams of about five students. Hot line teams can be important, because often students have few resources to call upon to help them to do their homework; many parents are unable or unwilling to help their children. Often middle class parents hire tutors to help their children to become proficient in a given subject—something poor families cannot afford do.

Students often become frustrated with homework; when this happens, they have trouble settling down to do their homework because they know that no help is forthcoming. A team of five or so competent students can be selected weekly to be available to help others with their homework.

This student team will be on call to answer questions and help their fellow students with homework by phone. Each student in the class is given a list of the names and phone numbers of the hot line team. Eventually, computers will replace the hot line; home computers will be connected with one other to make it possible for all students to participate in computer conferencing. Although such technology now exists, it has not yet been widely enough disseminated for most students to use.

Another way to get students to utilize their resources is to divide all students in class into teams, with each team having a coordinator. The coordinator should be rotated, so no one person feels permanently stuck with the job. The coordinator of each team is responsible for prodding students to do both in-class and homework assignments. These coordinators should be students who are competent to help others with their work. Team coordinators should be proactive; they should call those who have a history of failing to do their homework to see if they can be of help and to encourage them to get their work done.

In an instance like this, grading should not be done on a curve; all students should get As if they do competent work. Periodic feedback should be given to the class, so everyone can see how well they have improved.

Action Questions

How would you go about setting up a homework hot line? How long would students be expected to serve on the hot line team at a given time? What's your rationale for this? How would you rotate them? What would be the reward for students being on the hot line team?

How could you use retired school teachers or professors or other elderly volunteers to participate in your homework hot line? Is this a feasible idea? How could you set this up? What are the hindering forces you expect to encounter? What are the likely supporting forces?

How would you go about setting up coordinators to manage teams for your classes? How long would students be expected to be team coordinators? How would you rotate them? What would be the reward system for students to be coordinators? How would you respond to parents complaining that their child spends too much time helping other students in class with their homework?

How would you evaluate the effectiveness of the management teams? How would you evaluate the overall effectiveness of class performances?

What would you anticipate would be the reaction of other teachers and administrators to the team coordinator approach? What hindering forces can you expect? What supporting forces?

What other ways can you use students as resources to help each other achieve?

Child Development

Because a great number of "babies are having babies" in our modern society, our schools need to explore ways to educate against and break this and other aspects of the cycle of poverty and dependency that often cuts across generations. Parents who are in their teens seldom have the necessary emotional and physical development, let alone the educational background, to be effective parents.

While instruction in sex education and AIDS awareness are critical, instruction in child development may be equally appropriate. Such a course would not only focus on the needs and developmental stages of childhood, but also on the costs involved in terms of food, clothing, shelter, and education, and the time, energy, and patience it takes to be a good parent. Topics such as prevention of child abuse, the impact of drugs and poor diet both during pregnancy and while rearing children, and legal aspects of parethood could well be covered.

A Scenario

Another important area for consideration in such instruction is that of modern gender roles. What does it mean to be a man, to be a woman? In what ways have the definitions of gender changed in recent years? By focusing on gender roles, might our instruction have some positive impact on how students relate one to another? Examples might be to have students consider and compare such media icons as the Huxstible family from the *Cosby Show* and Doughboy and Trev from *Boys in the Hood*, or the family from *Different Strokes* with their own neighbhood experiences.

There are some schools that emphasize parenting by having students assigned to male-female pairs, with each pair given a doll or an egg to care for as if it were a living infant. The students are to take turns carrying and caring for this "infant" during the school day and after school, as a subject for classroom discussion and analysis.

Action Questions

What possibilities do such activities have? What experiences have you had with such educational efforts?

Would a course in child development be useful in your school? What topics should be included in such a class? How would you go about organizing a course of that type?

How would you get support for such a course from the school administstgration? From the community? How would you respond to parents who feel such a course is unnecessary, or even an intrusion into their responsibilities as parents? What other questions might come up in such considerations?

The Political Context

Given the information explosion of recent decades, enhanced by the expanding technologies of newspapers, television, radio, and computers, the modern world now enjoys the experiencing of news almost as fast as the events being reported happen. Things that take place halfway around the world are reported alongside those that take place next door. Even though we are often overwhelmed with such information, the evolution of information technology continues at an accelerating rate. The world has most certainly become that "global village" so often mentioned.

Obviously, as information and the ability to communicate it expands, it is not possible to teach all worthwhile information. There is not enough time in the school day, the school year, indeed in a lifetime. Curriculum decisions must be made in all schools, based upon questions of what is important for teachers to teach and for students to learn. Many, many topics must be left out. How are such decisions made? Are these strictly educational decisions, or are they also political in nature?

In many schools across the United States, the offering of an African American studies course is not seen as a high priority. As school officials wrestle with the wide range of available information, and the problem of how to fit as much as possible into the curriculum, something like African American studies is seen as either unnecessary or counterproductive.

Yet, this question may be approached in a different manner. Given the contemporary and future information explosion, it is no longer feasible to create a curriculum of facts to be learned. Rather, the purpose of school must be to learn how to learn, so that today's students will be able to deal with a wide range of knowledge that is not yet available to them, or to any of us. It is a matter of problem solving, or learning how to define situations, where to go for information, and how to piece it all together. All of this requires a social and political context.

Two contemporary educators, Benjamin Bloom and Paulo Freire, offer some important principles for teaching all youngsters today, and particularly African American youngsters. It is not only important for students to learn problem-solving and how to learn, but it is vital that they acquire such skills with an understanding of the political and social realities in which they can use such skills.

Bloom states that it is important to teach structure rather than facts. By teaching structure, one helps students learn how to learn, and from where to retrieve information. When study skills were discussed earlier, it was suggested that the strategy of learning to read topic sentences was a key to getting the most out of each paragraph. This is a structural approach to written materials, and helps identify the source from which information can be retrieved. It not only increases the understanding of written materials and the manner in which such materials are structured, but also enhances one's reading and writing ability.

To be effective in educating African American children, teaching should be done within a political context that affirms the existence of those children, that raises their consciousness, that says that they are worthy and can be empowered to take charge of their lives and make a difference. Because of the predominance of white cultural hegemony, it is as if African American children fail to see their image when they observe themselves in a mirror. It is from this point of view that the value and significance of African American studies as an integral part of the curriculum is seen as important—as indeed a necessity. Such studies help provide African American children with a mirror image that is powerful and exciting; African American studies help build the self-concept of African American students.

Putting the process of education, of teaching both context and learning skills, in a form that strengthens the meaning of education for those being educated is the key. If education is to be empowering for all students, then political decisions must be part of curricular decisions, to assure that all relevant constituencies within the student body are being served.

Action Questions

What do you think the political context is in your school, in your school district? How should the curriculum be structured to be most relevant and meaningful to the students you are serving? What is necessary to properly empower those students? How should the overall educational program be constructed?

Do you anticipate resistance if you were to move in the directions suggested by such political circumstances? Would there be support for such directions? What kinds of support would you need?

Importance of Skills

This section has involved a review of some potential strategies through which schools can better focus on the acquisition of basic skills by all students. The manner in which the curriculum is structured, the use of instructional interventions such as a three-year cycle, the utilization of cross-age tutoring, and of computers, are just some of the possibilities to be explored.

You are urged to raise yet other topics and possibilities, with the understanding that the school program cannot be considered successful unless all of the students are acquiring the basic skills they will need to enter the adult world and be able to continue to learn as that world changes.

Notes

Criteria V:
Monitoring of Pupil Progress

The fifth criteria for effective schools suggested by Edmonds is the insistence that pupil progress be continually monitored in a manner that assures that all members of the educational team are constantly aware of pupil progress in relationship to instructional objectives.

To assure that effective education of all students is taking place as desired, it is necessary for each school and each classroom to develop procedures that will foster overall monitoring of academic progress.

Some considerations and techniques which may help such efforts are as follows.

Quality Circles

The use of quality circles (QCs), in which teachers meet at least weekly to discuss and seek solutions to educational problems, provides an excellent forum for sharing information on instructional plans and monitoring overall student progress. QCs are a management tool developed in industry, and one that can be implemented in schools without threatening the authority of the principal (Bryant, 1988). QCs are a means to break down barriers within a school organization and encourage improvement by allowing time for teachers within that organization to get together in small groups to engage in problem solving.

The effectiveness of QCs in any setting will depend upon the commitment of the people involved and the leadership that evolves from the discussion. Although the QC technique is not new, or even particularly innovative, it has for the most part not been used in the school setting. It appears, nonetheless, to have considerable promise as a method of decreasing the isolation that classroom teachers often feel.

Through voluntary meetings within the school schedule, teachers of the same grade level—or across grade levels—can be mutually supportive of each other, can profit from an exchange of ideas on curriculum and instructional procedures, and can address the needs of the students with respect to monitoring of progress, development of discipline, and improvement of teaching.

While QCs are not something new or mystical, since the concept is deeply rooted in behavioral science literature, implementation of this approach may not be as simple as it might appear. Organizations of all kinds, including schools, are often wedded to traditional hierarchical forms of management, and the QC approach runs counter to that tradition. For QCs to be used effectively, the principal and other school leaders will need to be willing to provide time for teachers to get together, and allow an opportunity for teachers to try out new ideas that evolve from the QC discussions.

A Scenario

Consider, for example, that as a school administrator you have managed to free up two hours each week for teachers to meet by grade level in QCs. Based on your years of experience, you have concluded that the effective management of a school is more than a one-person job, and you want to involve your teachers not only in solving and monitoring educational problems, but also in decision making about the overall operation of the school.

You hope that having teachers come together in QCs will allow them to build a support system that will be of assistance to you and of value to the school. Unfortunately, as you propose the idea to your teaching staff, it is apparent that many of the teachers are resisting the idea.

Action Questions

Why would there be such resistance on the part of teachers? What can you do to overcome such resistance? What other problems might occur in the implementation of QCs in a school? What could be done in a situation where teachers wanted such a process, but the administration did not?

What are some of the topics that QCs might best deal with in a school? In particular, how might QCs be used to develop and enhance overall monitoring of academic progress?

Action Research

Another way in which teachers in the school setting can better address the question of monitoring student progress is through the implementation of action research. Teachers will need to change the traditional concept of themselves as simple technicians, guided by the content of textbooks, readers, and other such tools.

Instead, they must see themselves, at least in part, as researchers who will identify, diagnose, and study the academic problems of their students, and build curricula and instructional plans based upon such new data.

A successful program of action research in a classroom or school will result in a better understanding of the educational needs of the students and the creation of an academic program focused to overcome whatever educational deficiencies are identified. If an action research program is closely tied to the monitoring of student progress, it can help all professionals in the school keep their eyes on the goal of helping all students learn effectively.

The action research model consists of planning, action, observation, and evaluation. It is a model that is not based upon a random sample or other traditional quantitative research methodologies, but rather upon a problem that needs to be solved; therefore, what an action researcher learns about the instruction of a particular child may not have transferability to other children, nor is it intended to.

Neither is action research dependent upon past findings; such data may not be that relevant or helpful in any or every particular situation. The most important point in action research is that, through a repetitive cycle of planning, action, observation, and evaluation, problems can be solved and improvements can be made in the educational program, student by student, and class by class. An action researcher may go through this repetitive cycle a half dozen times or more before a solution to a particular problem is found.

Action Questions

Given your experience as a teacher, consider how you

have, or might in the future, use action research to assist your students. What are the possibilities? What are the problems involved?

What resistance would you expect to the use of action research in your school? How would you defend its use? What do you see as its advantages and disadvantages?

Group Lesson Plans

Another procedure for school-wide monitoring of student progress is the use of group lesson plans. Teachers have been trained for generations to function in an isolated manner, with attention only to what is occurring in their individual classrooms. If we are to better address the needs of all students, and particularly to improve the academic performance of disadvantaged and minority students, we need to break away from this isolation and develop a unified approach to instructional activities in our schools.

Under a group lesson plan system, each teacher must know not only what he or she is doing within the single classroom, but also what one's colleagues are doing in other classrooms in the school. The instruction in basic skills must be coordinated to assure that all students are being provided with the necessary academic tools, and the instructional content must be consistent enough to assure that no student will lack the knowledge required to move forward in school.

Such group lesson plan activities should also foster a consistent approach to student discipline and classroom management, so that students will know better what to expect and what is expected of them.

Released time will need to be provided in order for teachers to meet in small groups, discuss their classroom procedures and plans, and create a group lesson plan system. A commitment to the value of this approach must exist both from the principal and among the participating teachers. Group lesson plans are one possible outgrowth of using QCs in a school.

Action Questions

Consider some of the major issues to be addressed in developing group lesson plans. What would such group plans look like in your school? Would the teachers find such an approach interesting? Threatening? Desirable?

What support would be needed from the principal and other school or district administrators? What sort of time would be needed to make such a system work? How can such plans be used to monitor student performance?

Developing New Materials

Utilization of QCs, action research, and group lesson plans, either singly or together, requires movement on the part of the participating teachers away from the technician mode mentioned previously. All of these new techniques suggest that the teachers will be, both individually and as a group, a creative force within the school.

The technician role into which many if not most teachers have fallen historically is, at least in part, a result of the dominant role that publishing companies have come to play through decisions made with respect to which instructional materials and textbooks will be available. As the role of the publishers has increased, teachers have been left with fewer and fewer choices in the way of materials that might meet the particular needs of their students or the specific manner in which they might want to teach a particular subject.

While it is true that it is not economically feasible for publishing companies to produce as wide a range of materials as might be desired by all teachers or might be needed for each and every unique community within our nation, the fact that desired materials are not available in the form of commercial textbooks or workbooks does not mean that teachers should necessarily make do with what is commercially produced.

Through QC discussion, through action research in the classroom and school, and through the development of group lesson plans, teachers in every school can identify the kinds of specific materials that they desire, and in cases where such materials are not available from publishers, the teachers should move to develop their own instructional materials. Given recent developments in computers and desk-top publishing techniques, the creation of educational materials is today both fairly easy and inexpensive.

As educators, we need to have the best interests of our students at hand. If available textbooks fail to address the needs of African American students, or any other students individually or by group, then teachers need to write and create their own materials. This can be one of the tasks identified through QCs, and for which time can be made available within the teacher's work day.

Researching student needs and writing curriculum materials to address those needs will allow teachers to graduate from being mere instructional technicians to being real teachers—in both a creative and political sense. It is an act that breaks away from the educational conformity instituted by the publishing houses and the national curriculum committees, and it is an act of empowerment for both teachers and students in the local community. By using the children's own experiences and community setting as a base for new educational materials, the teachers will provide a spirit of liberation and meaning to the act of schooling.

A Scenario

Consider a situation in which you are a history teacher in a racially integrated school, and you find that the history books purchased by the school system do not do justice to the role of African American people in shaping America. You have complained to the principal many times, as well as to the social studies department head, but no new books have been forthcoming.

Now you inform them that you will be creating your own history materials. Their response is that the school district has spent a considerable amount of taxpayer money on the books that it has, and that you are expected to use them.

Action Questions

How would you respond to this scenario? What would you say to the principal and the department head? How do you make the case that the textbooks are inadequate, that you cannot properly instruct you students about the role of African Americans without materials that focus appropriately on that subject?

As a teacher or administrator, how can you get teachers to be less dependent on textbooks? How can you encourage them to develop independent materials? What kind of support do you need, in terms of time, funds, and administrative assistance? Will teachers working together on such projects be more successful, more effective? How would you monitor student progress when using locally developed and produced materials?

Standardized Tests

Not only are nationally developed and normed standardized tests one of the means available for monitoring student progress, but in nearly every school, every school district, and every state, such tests are mandated at various points during the educational process.

For decades now, there has been a debate raging over the use of such tests and the judging of all students in the same manner. It is well recognized that such nationally normed tests are culturally biased in favor of the dominant white western culture, that such tests discriminate against African American children, Hispanic children, Native American children, and other racial and cultural minorities who do not share to the same degree the dominant patterns measured in such instruments. Year in and year out, minority children fail to do as well on such examinations.

Such test results have had several negative affects on American education. They have served to reinforce the stereotypes held by many teachers that minority students do not do as well in school. They have been used to categorize, group, and track African American and other minority students in inferior educational programs, thus serving as conveyor belts to the inferior jobs in society, or to unemployment and poverty.

Despite these problems, it seems clear that standardized testing is so ingrained into our educational system that rather than try to get rid of it, we must find ways to use it to the advantage of all children. Many will argue that teaching students specifically to pass or succeed at certain standardized tests is not really education, that it only teaches what is on the test. Yet, if such tests serve as the entry into other educational opportunities—into the mainstream of American life—then teaching students to pass such hurdles may be highly appropriate. For if African American students continue to fail at these tests, which have life-long political and economic effects that otherwise thwart future opportunities and minimize future choices, nothing good has been served by ignoring such realities.

The 1960s was an era of visible forms of race and class struggle, of recognizing and seeking to alleviate educational and social problems, of examining ways in which the schools could be used to accomplish such goals. Many of those battles continue to be waged in the 1990s. One form of that ongoing struggle is to find ways to make all aspects of schooling equally available and effective for all students.

If standardized tests are to be used to judge educational achievement and potential, to admit students to future educational opportunities, then in

order to empower all students, we must be sure that they are all trained to handle and master such examinations. Those tests are the new battleground of the class and economic struggle.

If the political economy of standardized testing is a reality in our schools, then those educators who work with disadvantaged and minority students, and particularly with African American students, must in every class in every grade focus on the basic skills and knowledge that will appropriately prepare their students for such tests.

Action Questions

What are some of the educational issues involved in teaching students to do well on standardized tests? How do the test-taking services train students, and which of these techniques could be used in the public school classroom?

How can teachers help students understand the importance of such tests? What forms of assistance are needed and which of them might be obtained from outside the school?

Continual Monitoring

Through these procedures and others that you will identify and utilize, it should be possible for teachers and administrators at any school to be continually aware of the progress being made by each and every student in that school. By keeping an eye on such educational results, and by altering the instructional approach and materials to maximize student progress, you will be making important strides toward operating an effective school for all children.

Notes

Conclusion

The five criteria for effective schooling, as espoused by Edmonds, are well known and have been generally highly regarded in American education since he and others articulated them in the late 1970s. The many educational strategies suggested here as appropriate means of seeking to implement Edmond's criteria, while not new in most cases, are, in the main, untested in schools.

These ideas are not proposed here as sure-fire cures to contemporary educational problems. Rather, all educators are encouraged to approach their classrooms and schools in an innovative manner, with a willingness to try new ideas and seek ways to reach all students.

In the final decade of the Twentieth Century, marked by a continuing torrent of educational reports suggesting that our schools are in deep trouble, most of our educational leaders argue that we are on the road to "reform." The ideas that began with the *A Nation at Risk* report have stirred a renewed interest in educational basics, an increase in graduation requirements of many schools, and intense attention to international competition in education as well as commerce.

Yet, with all this flurry of "reform," evidence documents that African American students in particular, and minority and disadvantaged students in general, are not doing better educationally. The genuinely "at risk" portion of our so-called "nation at risk" has not yet been helped by the contemporary educational "reforms." It is estimated that perhaps 70 percent of American students have benefitted from these new school initiatives, but that the other 30 percent, the disadvantaged and minority population of our schools in general, has not been positively impacted (Reinhold, 1987).

Thus, it is left to the individual teachers and school administrators, on a school-by-school basis across the nation, to make educational reform real for all of their students. The challenge is greatest for those who teach and lead schools with significant proportions of minority students, with students who by measures of family income and other indices fall outside the mainstream of American culture.

Yet, if we are to avoid even greater educational and social problems in the future, the education of all of our children is a challenge that must be met in the immediate future. It is to this end that we have offered these suggestions for new educational considerations and approaches for teaching in schools and classrooms serving African American students. We encourage all teachers and school administrators to find ways to reach all of their students, to commit themselves to liberate all youngsters with the necessary skills and knowledge to be successful.

Notes

References

Bloom, B. *Taxonomy of Educational Objectives: The Classification of Educational Goals.* New York: McKay Company, 1974.

Bryant, B. *Quality Circles: New Management Strategies for Schools.* Ann Arbor, MI: Prakken Publications, 1988 (Distributed by Gaddo Gap Press, San Francisco, CA).

Canter, L. and M. Canter. *Assertive Discipline.* Santa Monica, CA: Canter and Associates, Inc., 1987.

Edmonds, R. Some Schools Work and More Can. *Social Policy,* March/April 1979.

Edmonds, R., and J. Frederiksen. *Search for Effective Schools: The Identification and Analysis of City Schools that Are Instructionally Effective for Poor Children.* Cambridge, MA: Center for Urban Studies, 1978.

Erlandson, D. *Strengthening School Leadership.* Danville, IL: Interstate Printers, 1976.

Friere, P. *Pedagogy of the Oppressed.* New York: The Seabury Press, 1974.

Gathercoal, F. *Judicious Discipline* (Third Edition). San Francisco, CA: Caddo Gap Press, 1993.

Hilliard, A. *Improving School Climate: Leadership Techniques for Education.* Reston, VA: National Association of School Principals, 1980.

Kiewra, K. Acquiring Effective Notetaking Skills: An Alternative to Professional Notetaking. *Journal of Reading,* 1984, 299-302.

Kiewra, K. Learning from a Lecture: An Investigation of Notetaking, Review, and Attendance at a Lecture. *Human Learning,* 1985, 4, 73-77.

Kiewra, K., and Benton, S. L. The Relationship Between Information-Processing Ability and Notetaking. *Contemporary Educational Psychology,* 1988, 13, 33-44.

Kleinsmith, L. A Computer-Based Biology Study Center: Preliminary Assessment of Impact. Ann Arbor, MI: University of Michigan, unpublished paper, 1987.

Madden, J., D. Lawson, and D. Sweet. *School Effectiveness Study.* Sacramento, CA: State Department of Education, 1976.

National Commission for Excellence in Education. *A Nation at Risk.* Washington, D.C.: U.S. Government Printing Office, 1983.

Palmer, P. *To Know as We Are Known: A Spirituality of Education.* San Francisco, CA: Harper and Row, 1983.

Reinhold, R. School Reform: 4 Years of Tumult, Mixed Results. *New York Times,* August 10, 1987.

Wayne State University College of Education. *School Dropouts in Michigan: A Report to the State Legislature and a Proposal for the Review and Study of School Dropouts.* Lansing, MI: Michigan Department of Education, 1987.

About the Authors

Bunyan Bryant, a faculty member with the School of Natural Resources at the University of Michigan in Ann Arbor, has for two decades taught courses, undertaken research, and conducted workshops and special programs to identify, understand, and seek correction of inequalities in American education. He holds a Ph.D. in education and an M.S.W. degree in social work from the University of Michigan and a B.S. degree from Eastern Michigan University, where he majored in social science with minors in biology and psychology.

While serving as a research project director at the Institute for Social Research of the University of Michigan in the 1960s and 1970s, Bryant designed and executed action research projects with school systems experiencing racial conflict. As a faculty member in the School of Natural Resources, he teaches courses in environmental advocacy and coordinates research which has identified the frequency with which hazardous waste is disposed at sites located in minority communities.

Bryant serves frequently as a consultant to schools in Detroit and other urban areas and to environmental action organizations across the nation. He is also the author of four other books, including *Quality Circles: New Management Strategies for Schools,* and co-editor along with Paul Mohai of *Race and the Incidence of Environmental Hazards: A Time for Discourse.*

Alan H. Jones is publisher at Caddo Gap Press in San Francisco, California. He is the editor of *Teacher Education Quarterly,* publisher of *Multicultural Education,* the magazine of the National Association for Multicultural Education, and an editorial and publishing consultant to several other educational associations and agencies. He holds a B.A. degree in social science, an M.A. degree in international education, and a Ph.D. degree in social foundations of education, all from the University of Michigan.

Jones has served as a junior high school teacher, a university faculty member and department chair in teacher education and the social foundations of education, a state education consultant and bureau chief, an educational association executive, and in several editing and publishing roles in the field of education. He has also served as president of the American Educational Studies Association and is curently the Secretary-Treasurer of the Council of Learned Societies in Education.

Jones has served as author and editor of numerous books, monographs, and articles in the field of education, including *Civic Education for Teachers: The Capstone for Educational Reform.*